Thinking in the Cloud

and

Other Poems from Upstairs

Philip Wadner
2015

Published by Cade Books

ISBN 978-0-9931987-2-4

www.cadebooks.co.uk

Contents

Introduction

Sestina, pantoum, rondelet,
Poetic forms in wide array.
An ode, perhaps haiku as well,
A thought provoking villanelle
Or sonnet, nonnet, clerihew.
For formalists nought else will do!

But if it's not a special treat
Or makes your heart forget a beat,
Produces sniffs and teary eyes
Or maybe tummy butterflies,
What use is strict poetic form
If all it does is spawn a yawn?

So settle down, indulge with me
This little book of poetry.

Busy Bees

You know how people say they can't sit still?
It makes me wonder if perhaps they're ill.
There's nothing wrong with staring at a wall
Or doing absolutely nothing at all.

Where is the virtue in being full of beans
And rushing to complete the day's routines?
Switch on the kettle, brew a dark espresso,
The jobs to do will still be there tomorrow.

Do cows rush down the field at milking time
Or clocks speed up between their hourly chime?
Lay back and close your eyes, all will be well.
You have no need to join life's carousel.

Consider, it's only yourself you need to please
So leave the stress to others: the busy bees.

Death by Tinnitus

Ear worm, what pleasures do you find
inside my head? Your constant hiss
like steam, when all around is quiet.
To wake in silence is just a dream.

Your autumn rustle all year through,
with tuning strings perpetual
cacophony. A prison term,
a life of jangling symphony.

Like ocean waves on shingled shore
ensnared within an empty conch
to dance, with dream-world music spinning
rapidly in abstract trance.

Must flee this never ending shriek
that fuddles minds from deep inside
one's ear with constant clamour. Might
you be the final sound I hear?

A Sticky End

A mouse. A mouse is in the house!
It kept awake my sleepy spouse
And ate our cheese, the little louse
With more than ample share of nous,
That cheeky mouse.

Oh no! Our mouse has turned to mice,
Not one, not two, but mouses thrice.
They're in the sugar, in the rice,
They're everywhere to be precise,
Those pesky mice!

And now we have a mouse quartet.
They've played some jazz, not well just yet.
We heard them jam a rhythm set
On drums, trombone and gold trumpet.
A funky mousy minuet.

The noise attracted dear old Smudge.
As felines go, he's quite a drudge,
But only needs the gentlest nudge
To know when something has to budge.
Turns mice to fudge.

The Old Schoolroom

Orange pens with scratchy nibs well-stained with ink
from china pots filled up from spouted kettles,
and wooded handles chewed to help us think
of places, dates and queens and kings and battles.

With powder painted pictures on the door
of Mum and Dad by George, aged six and a quarter,
a crate of empty bottles on the floor,
and beans in jars that looked in need of water.

Long shelves of books to learn to read and write
and spell, geography to be discussed.
And sticks of chalk, all lengths, in blue and white,
the blackboard grey from history lesson's dust.

Those beans in jars that as young kids we sowed,
like us grew tall, to travel life's long road.

Grandparents

Ash flecks blotch her weary skirt
From cigarettes nipped by tan-stained lips.
She coughs her way through washing shirts
And sheets, and pressing pillowslips.
A long way down my family tree,
Which part of her is me?

Fifteen hours, day is done,
Fingers gnarled by working loam.
Sore crackled skin from scorching sun
While carrying the harvest home.
A long way down my ancestry,
Which part of him is me?

Drum Major, engineer, disposed
To Belgium in the First World War.
Tuberculosis diagnosed,
Lost, not to battle, thirty four.
A long way down my pedigree,
Which part of him is me?

Fox cape on shoulders, gold-pinned cloche,
Sweet Parma Violet under tongue.
Soprano voice flowed with panache,
An angel, heroine unsung.
In my sea of genealogy,
Which part of her is me?

Dear Old Soul

Soggy stockings, soles flopping, charity shop hopping.

Pension day, bills to pay,
Rooms to heat, no food to eat,
Little left to shoe her feet.

Colour? Uncaring, so long as they're wearing.
Navy or black, or fawn, or brown.
The uppers, some fine, but the heels are well down.

Leather, rubber, plastic soles,
Some intact and some with holes.
Scuffed and worn, frayed and torn,
Some polished like new, but only a few.

They no longer fit, or the fashion has passed,
Only worn once and out they are cast.
Ladies' and girls', gentlemen's, earls',
Inserts with curls, buttons with pearls.
And not too expensive, to boot.

How much are these? Do they suit?

The Wireless Set

Hissy fits and snaps and spits,
Batteries big as boxer's fists.
Accumulated grease and grime
Holds memories from another time.

Knobs and buttons Bakelite,
Tuning dial lights up bright.
Search for stations, only hum,
Where on earth *is* Hilversum?

Smoky stains and finger smudges,
Switch it on and no-one budges.
Family sat around the set
To hear a play, or string quartet.

The Archers, Goons and Mrs Dale,
The Navy Lark, beyond the pale.
Family Favourites, Down Your Way,
Music While You Work each day.

Evocative of bygone years,
But now collector's souvenirs,
The wireless sets no longer play.
Their dulcet tones now yesterday.

Snow Chap

Want another drink, my dear?
Said the snow chap to his wife.
I can't stand up, she answered back,
I'm in a bit of strife.

Must have been that Gin and It
That made me kind of dizzy.
I should have had a cup of tea
Or something that was fizzy.

I'll help you up the snow chap said
Well hurry, she replied.
My bottom's gone all mushy, and
I'm falling on my side.

You'll catch your death just laying there.
The snowman looked quite sad.
He scratched the carrot on his face
and said it's not too bad.

It's not too bad? she shouted back,
With both my arms unfreezing?
It feels as though they're dropping off,
and now I feel like sneezing.

Best not do that, the snow chap said
'Cos just a little cough
could make you shatter, then we'll see
your buttons shooting off.

The snow girl said, I say old chap
I wish you'd stop your whining.
Just come and help me straighten up
Before the sun starts shining.

And could you get a bottle please?
It would be rather nice
To have another drink, I think.
Don't bother with the ice.

The snow chap said I'll sort things out,
Being quite a clever geezer.
Just wait a mo and I'll be back.
I'm off to get the freezer.

There is no need, my dear old chap,
Said snow girl, face aglow.
I'm nicely icing up again.
The weather's back to snow!

To Mother

(From Whittingham Asylum, October 1948)

You know why I'm here, buried under a cloud,
With nothing but shame left at home, as it seems
You denied them the truth when I told it out loud.

Even though on my grandmother's life I avowed,
It was taken as lying, and put down to dreams.
You know why I'm here, buried under a cloud.

I asked for a candle, was never allowed
As I laid in the dark and recalled wicked schemes.
You denied them the truth when I told it out loud.

Can't stand this much longer; I've told them just how'd
End my life, maybe drowning in one of the streams.
You know why I'm here, buried under a cloud.

I've signed myself out from this discarded crowd,
But no-one believes I could go to extremes.
You denied them the truth when I told it out loud.

He's my father; I know that you need to stand proud
But I cannot believe you ignored all my screams.
You know why I'm buried here, under a cloud.
You denied them the truth when I told it out loud.

Our Daily Bread

(A themed collection of five sonnets)

Six o'clock

As slumber's shadow slips away at dawn
And sleep surrenders, silent but the birds
That shrill their song through heavy drapes still drawn
To shake the world awake with joyous words,

A bargain's struck with warmth beneath the quilt:
Just let me lie with you a moment more
Before my sea of thought and notion's spilt
And shipwrecked dreams are tossed upon the shore.

While streaks of sun crack through the heavy cloth
And weave the break of day into my eyes,
I wrestle to fight off the night's behemoth
And wipe the crumbs from Sandman's enterprise.

The day awaits and sleep will have to hold
Until tonight I steal beneath the folds.

Eight o'clock

Laid hopefully, by corn fed speckled hens
From open fields, wide skies and feathered clouds,
Cracked open, hope abandoned, no amen,
Two golden suns, their yolks domed tall and proud.

Sharp pangs of hunger needing to be sated
To break the famine of the shadowed hours.
With earth-sweet tang, and craving unabated,
I muse: could sense of smell alone devour?

No sooner thought, albumen turns to white,
And oblate orbs glide, grudging, from the pan.
The suns explode beneath my knife, despite
A final struggle, animal and man.

With stomach filled and hunger put at bay
The morning lies ahead, a bright bouquet.

Twelve o'clock

While shadows shorten under summer sun,
I'm sensing that it's time to stoke the coals
Whose embers have been dying through the morn,
And slay this burning need to feed my soul.

A fragrant spice creeps out from under doors
And calls to me like sands reach out to tide.
My stomach growls that way one can't ignore
And drives me to discover that inside.

Above the blare a distant chime spells twelve.
Decision done the doors give way to thrust
As instincts pull me in to dig and delve
Where steaming Chim Chum vies with grilled langouste.

With belly stretched and shirtfront almost rent,
My appetite is, once again, content.

Five o'clock

The evening breeze blows soft to stir the air.
Once bustling hives, the workers leave the town
To dawdlers loitering without a care
And seeking sweet allure the devil's sown.

A teashop window boasts enticing treats
Of tempting, dark, delicious cacao dreams
That fudge the mind, my heart forgets its beat
And ripples down ambrosial chocolate streams.

Lunch long since eaten, dreams will not fulfil
This eagerness for sweetness in my brain.
With opened purse I give away all will,
To swirl in sensual cream and frangipane.

Like first love's thrill, my eager tongue caressed,
Dark nectar lays my troubled mind to rest.

Eleven o'clock

At last, the time to crawl back into bed,
Yet, even though the day's been filled with food,
The yearning for a dream-filled night ahead;
Best china, snow white tablecloths bestrewed

With dishes, varied as the time of day,
My alimentary canal cries out
For gourmet spread from filet through flambé.
Like raging thirst in midst of summer drought,

It wails aloud for further nourishment
With thunderous clamour clawing at my ears,
Foreboding cries that threaten to torment
And browbeat guardians of night's frontiers.

Like borborygmic plumbing, impolite,
My stomach grunts a gruffled groan.
'Goodnight'.

Cacao Dream

Chocolate
Cup Cake
Dark and daring, delectable devil's dough,
play your sweet lure, soft sensual sponge.
Titillating, teasing, tempting, top to toe.
Icing, inciting intimacy, yield to tongue!
Magnificent, inimitable, iniquitous scent.
Crème de la crème, chocolate suspense.
Caress my nose with your rich accent.
Burst on my buds, sate every sense.
Melt from mouth to my heart.
Paint a chocolate stream
of culinary art.
Cacao dream.

The Festive Porker

Pork pies come, and pork pies go,
And most pork pies are just so-so.
But this pork pie, to say the least,
Was quite a gastronomic feast!

Six inches tall, and twice as wide
This pie home-made for Christmastide.
A family spread without a doubt,
Our crusty bake of snout throughout.

Out of the fridge (still on the plate)
With carving knife to orchestrate.
A squeal slipped out, and someone said,
'You sure that piggy's really dead?'

We cut it up in regal portion
Not heeding dietary caution.
It slid down easy into belly
Helped along by sloppy jelly.

Most was eaten up for tea
And shared around the family,
But one wedge of this rarity
Was frozen for posterity.

The Village Hall

On Sunday mornings, WI have Bring and Buy,
unwanted clothes and bric-a-brac,
With tea in china pots a-brewing and apple pie
in plenty, for a hearty snack.

Alternate weeks on Mondays the hall committee
pontificates with lengthy abundance
About how much should still be in the kitty
with everyone talking at once.

Tuesday evening's Zumba, girls with curls
and rhythmic prancing to the beat
With twists and turns and jumps and yells, and twirls
which blur their feet.

Wednesday evening quiz night draws the crowds,
keen to show how much they know
Of sports and books, and ports and cooks and clouds,
and matters apropos.

On every second Thursday through the year
the hall is filled with sobriety.
The History Society meet to hear
of local notoriety.

Friday's slimming, yoga, book club vie
for space in different nooks
For diets, lotus poses, pages wrung dry
from analysing books.

A wedding fills the hall some Saturdays
with happy pair anew.
'To bride and groom!' the best man hefts his glass,
their friends and family too.

Although the roof is thin and bricks are green
with mildew and decay,
The spirit that the village hall beholds
will never drift away.

Ladies Who Lunch

First on one cheek then the other,
Like courting swans they kissed the air.
Four ladies greeted one another
And called the waiter, 'Bill of Fayre!'
He had a hunch it was ladies who lunch.

They chatted over Chardonnay
While waiting for their favourite treat.
Some chicken filet, raspberry sorbet
(Window dressing, not to eat).
They didn't munch, those ladies who lunch.

One told of how she volunteers
For Meals on Wheels and things like that,
And had done so for many years.
A stifled yawn, no diplomat.
Well-practiced in scrunch, our ladies who lunch.

They pushed their food around for show
And touched each other's arms, engrossed
In other people's tales of woe.
To eminent friends they raised a toast.
A popular bunch, those ladies who lunch.

Our Char

Our Char was cooking a piece a
Some yummy Ital ee un pizza.
Her mum said 'What's that?
It'll make you too fat,
And then we shall have to decrease yer.'

Said our Char, 'But I'm really quite thin.'
As she started to break out a grin.
'And I know that my tummy's
Not crinkly like Mummy's,
And at least I am only six-tin.'

Well Mummy took umbrage and cried
'Til her nose was all runny inside.
'I promise, dear Charlotte
In future I shall not
Imply you are getting too wide.'

Don't Leave it Too Long

Dreams shredded
Secret love wedded
Clothes threaded
Bald headed.

I love yous unsaid
Regrets instead
Books unread
Sunsets in bed.

Neighbours ignored
Countries unexplored
Toasts not poured
Goals unscored.

Letters unsent
Missed life events
Money all spent
Out of date scent.

Tea cold
Shoes un-soled
Happiness on hold
Too old. Too old.

Squirrels

Endearing puffed out cheeks and large dark eyes,
The squirrel, stocky grey or leggy red
Chit chatters, softly meows or pierces cries
Through buck-teeth in appealing whiskered head.

Away from twiggy woods, in London Town,
Safe-cracking nuts from hangers filled for tits
While dangling gymnastically upside down.
Charming, clever, lithe acrobatics.

Statue-like he freezes, stooped and staring,
Twitching bush and tufted ears alert.
A sudden movement, in an act of daring
Grabs a nut, and scurries down to earth.

In parkour style he cuts a lively dash
To bury stocks of nuts. His winter cache.

Christmas Cake

Patricia baked a Christmas Cake,
'Twas full of fruit and butter.
'We want it now, we cannot wait.'
Her friends were heard to mutter.

But no, our Trisha had decreed
To wait 'til ten o'clock
Before she'd take her trusty knife
And cut them all a block.

The time arrived and up she shot!
Her friends all heard the crack.
'Oh no!', our Trisha shouted out,
'I've wrenched my flaming back!'

So down she sat and had a rest,
That was a big mistake.
An hour went by before she tried
Again to cut the cake.

By then the time was nigh eleven
And all their tums were rumbling.
They wanted cake and all they got
Was more of Trisha's fumbling.

She dropped the knife, it clattered down
And as she reached to catch it.
Another crack from Trisha's back,
A sound just like a ratchet.

'Oh no! I can't believe my luck.'
She wailed above the roaring.
Her friends were getting noisy now
As all their tums were gnawing.

'We'll cut the cake if you can't cope.'
The friends all rallied round.
But Trisha wouldn't budge an inch,
She just sat down and frowned.

'I brought it in, I'll do the biz.'
And with her eyes a-flare,
Our Trisha tried to stand again
And got up from her chair.

With grim resolve she gripped the knife,
Was over in a trice.
She closed her eyes, hoped for the best
And cut us all a slice.

Broken

My mind's a level crossing crash,
Twisted metal, smouldering ash.
Electric cables dangling, scrambled,
Neurons misfiring, thoughts entangled.

Counting numbers ceaselessly,
Forwards, backwards, needlessly.
One, two, three, four hundred, seven,
Thirty, twenty, twelve, eleven.

Agitated, addlepated,
Intellectually castrated.
Pages blank, no words at all,
Just hours staring at a wall.

Rainbows different shades of grey,
No winter snowdrops, bud-less May.
Birdsong hushed, no butterflies,
A hungry baby cries and cries.

Rustic bridges crossing streams
That used to bring idyllic dreams,
Now just an opportunity
To mend my constant misery.

Thinking in the Cloud

Been here before and seen the view,
It happens often, déjà vu,
Apparently out of the blue.
A place you never thought you knew.

Twins say they feel each other's pain,
A bond, a close ethereal chain.
They finish what the other's saying
As though they share a common brain.

An old friend who's been often greeted,
Name has gone, somewhere secreted.
You rack your brains, recall defeated.
It's accidentally been deleted?

Skydrive, OneDrive, Dropbox, Flickr
Facebook, Bebo, Tumblr, Twitter,
The Cloud's the place we go to fritter,
A kind of central neurotransmitter.

We use the Cloud to do our printing,
Perchance that's where we do our thinking.
No wonder our brains are slowly shrinking,
Our power of thought and inkling sinking.

Could be when memories overcrowd,
When words are locked up in a shroud,
When names cannot be said out loud,
Perhaps... we're thinking in the Cloud.

The Hidden Flower

Life is tough for you I know.
So many things go wrong, and yet
I wonder despite all the woe
You're not that empty silhouette.

That deep inside you're well at ease,
And happiness is round about
Like spring, after the winter freeze,
A crocus blooms, a snowdrop's out.

Although you hide behind a cloud
Of grey impenetrable gloom,
Force yourself to dump that shroud
And show the world your inner bloom.

The Green Cow

So many poems emphasise
The colours of their subject, so
Except in monochromatic guise,
How would a colour-blind poet know?

The sky we're told is usually blue.
For many though it's manifold,
From cobalt, red and pinkish hue
To milky white and morning gold.

The sea is quite a similar case,
Aquatic blue or ocean green
With grey tipped rollers interlaced,
And countless colours in-between.

But poetry comes from the heart,
Aesthetic, rhythmic, resonant.
Sensation is its counterpart;
Urgent, pregnant, incandescent.

It matters not that one might see
A cat that's pink, an orange horse,
And grazing on some sapphire lea
A herd of cows. All green, of course.

The Crystal Palace Fire

Four score and eight fire engines and their men
For long hours fought a battle to repel
The Crystal Palace nemesis, its tragedienne.
What use those water towers now, Brunel?

Like a cattle carcass on an ember bed,
Its bones licked clean by scorching blistering fire.
Lakes of cooling molten glass and lead
Conspired to flatten Paxton's deep desire.

The water towers stood tall above the haze,
Surveying twisted iron and melted glass.
With impatient disrespect the structure razed,
The towers the greatest stature there, alas.

A spark of engineering ingenuity
Extinguished in a firestorm of catastrophe.

Raclette Supper

Early evening coolness warmed by the granite stone,
Laughter fighting for position on the grill.
Pass the plate of chicken fillets if you will.

Raclette cheese melting over freshly peeled prawns,
New potatoes crushed with garlic cloves,
Buttered knobs from crusty homemade loaves.

Glasses clinking, Sauternes and Côtes du Rhône,
Sizzling sausages spitting as they grill,
Crunchy coleslaw zinged with chilli and dill.

Backdrop music mingling with blackbird's evening song,
Smiling faces lit by lilac twilight,
Soft conversation waning into the night.

Diet Rap

Too many visits to the refectory
Result in incapacity
And threaten mortality
Waistline fighting gravity
No vitality
Problem dietary
But who wants to live on celery
Or foods without a calorie
Or even worse, fat free
There must be an easier remedy
Ways to charge the battery
Make happy glands salivary
Without insanity
Or changing personality
But in reality
A diet rich in Kohlrabi
Offends the nerves olfactory
And visits to the lavatory
Become unsatisfactory
Just take more physicality
Start cooking with frugality
Don't fill up to capacity
Reduce your corporality
And potentiality
For fatality.

A Little Glass of Wine

You were a grape gripping to the vine,
Blushing in warm sunshine.
My own Chateau.
You were my little glass of wine.

You were sent by angels to shine,
A sparkling gemstone paradigm.
My Michelangelo.
You were my little glass of wine.

Some say it was intervention divine
That you agreed to be my Valentine.
My alpenglow.
You were my little glass of wine.

When you began to malign,
I failed to read the sign
And make you go.
You were my little glass of wine.

I should have drawn a line,
Had you wither on the vine,
But no.
I took another sip of my little glass of wine.

Total Eclipse

I don't see deep wrinkles, just creases from smiles
On a face that inspires, that enthrals and beguiles.
They're a sign of good humour, high spirits and cheers,
Of a person who's laughed a lot over the years.

I don't see grey hairs, just some lighter in shade
Than the tumbling tresses that used to cascade.
Golden strands softly wafted by light swells of air
Spinning shimmering shades of papaya and pear.

I don't see grey eyes, just the sparkling blue
That glistened in sunshine like heavenly dew.
That put me in mind of a coral reef sea,
Of an atoll surrounded by coconut trees.

I don't see two chins or pendulous breasts,
I don't hear knees creaking or short-winded chest,
I don't feel dried skin or kiss truculent lips.
Where age is concerned, love's a total eclipse.

Jazz Sextet

Crotchets jazz across the stage
To form a frenzied music rage,
While sharps and flats jerk semitones,
From energetic saxophones.

Double bass plucks rhythmic lows,
Delivering stomach thumping blows
Of palpable but subtle sound
In harmony, an octave down.

Bass drum kicked in syncopation,
Snare and side improvisation.
Brushes lightly scrub the skins
While top-hats crash, and cowbell tings.

Guitar alive with seventh chords
With dissonance enough to wake a corpse.
Plectrum flies across the strings
In rhythm with the jazzy swing.

Head hunched over ivories,
The pianist prioritises
Counterpoint from melody.
Quintessential irregularity.

Crotchets jazz across the page,
Resounding loudly off the stage.
The audience contentedly
Nod their heads in time, respectfully.

Haiku?

Haiku perhaps you
Mean a lot in Japanese
But you freeze me out.

Why do you exist
With seventeen syllables
That don't have to rhyme?

How much can be said
With so few words to embrace?
How much? Quite a lot!

Say a silent prayer
For people worse off than you
And see what ensues.

Suddenly you feel
The warmth of the summer sun
In winter's snow storms.

Suddenly you taste
The sweetest honeyed nectar
From bitter grapefruit.

Suddenly you see
A sea of smiling faces
Instead of sad tears.

Suddenly you smell
The fragrant flowers of spring
From dying roses.

Suddenly you hear
The sound of angels singing
From crying children.

Haiku, I get you.

Perpetuity

The wall clock clunks its steady beat,
Unchanging but for hourly chime
Which breaks the rhythm, to secrete
The ruthless marching on of time.

Unchanging but for hourly chime,
It sounds a million ticks to mark
The ruthless marching on of time,
From birth 'til when all light turns dark.

It sounds a million ticks to mark
The years, so short, though each day's long,
From birth 'til when all light turns dark,
When one chime plays our final song.

The years, so short, though each day's long
Which breaks the rhythm, to secrete
When one chime plays our final song.
The wall clock clunks its steady beat.

Summer's Song

No sooner do the days grow long
Than honey bees, with time to spare
Go window shopping, laissez faire,
Hypnotic with their droning song.

A blackbird pecks around the roots
Of fragrant shrubs and sundrenched flowers
Still fresh from unexpected showers,
To build her nest for new recruits.

Sunlight glints on ripples made
By trout, devouring water striders.
While anglers sip from mugs of cider,
Their floats dip under a willow's shade.

Airplane trails lace twilight hues
Like cotton wool balls strung up high,
Or fairy dust draped in the sky,
Or caterpillars on a sea of blue.

It seems no time since days grew long.
As trees cast off their russet dress,
Their branches bare of leafy flesh,
Nature fades out summer's song.

North Norfolk Coast

I never saw your summer blaze,
Preferring spring and autumn days
When sun sets soon across the sea
To paint The Wash in majesty.

Salt marshes edge the rugged coast,
And mud flats play a welcome host
To countless knot and common terns,
Returning to their summer homes.

Cold barren beaches stretch unending,
Where loneliness is unrelenting,
And tides ebb much too far to see
The edge of land, where sand meets sea.

A tranquil walk past flint-stone walls
Of seamen's houses, village hall,
A church, a friendly hostelry,
All steeped in Norfolk's history.

Nigh twenty years since I last saw
The beauty of North Norfolk's shore.
It lifts my heart to entertain
The thought I'll soon see you again.

Love

I have no need to touch your cheek
to feel the soft silkiness of your skin.

I have no need to breathe in the air
to smell your fragrant bouquet.

I have no need for appetite
to taste your ambrosial lips.

I have no need to turn my head and listen
to hear your silvery song.

I have no need to open my eyes
to see your enchanting smile.

I have no need.
Love is senseless.

Summer Bonnet Sonnet

Midsummer days, euphoric hours of heat
From sun-scorched sky, and thirty three degrees,
Bring wide brimmed hats endowed with flora, sweet
Pink fuchsia, felicia, and blossom from cherry trees.

Amid asparagus fern and fountain grass
Sway golden trumpets stalked by bumble bees,
With giddy jasmine turning heads that pass
The fragrance floating on the gentle breeze.

White rosebuds wave to passing papillons
Cavorting madly around the silky rim.
Red Admirals play chase between the fronds,
Resplendent, assiduous, spiritual seraphim.

Should hats express devotion, love so true,
This summer bonnet's sent from me to you.

By the same author:

Three Courses
Short Stories from Creative Writing Modules

This anthology of short stories brings together some of the author's recent writing, featuring an impressive combination of genres, techniques and styles.
Fifteen stories present the reader with a diverse cocktail of subject matter including hidden undercurrents in human relationships, humour, revenge and heartbreak. For dessert, the author has included ten microfiction stories, each one a complete tale and told in less than 250 words.
This eclectic mix should have something to please most tastes.

Whomerley Wood Moat, Stevenage - The House in the Clearing

Believed to have been the home of the de Homeley family in the late thirteenth century, the site of the medieval moated homestead in Whomerley Wood, Stevenage is located about one and a half miles almost due south of the original Saxon settlement around where St. Nicholas Church stands today. Evidence of medieval life has been found there, and excavations on the island have also uncovered relics from Roman times. The author has sifted through a huge variety of sources, and has knitted together facts, suppositions and his personal reflections to create a powerful image of times gone by.

Probate - A Personal Journey

After a sad family bereavement, I started out on what I thought could be a lengthy and arduous process of obtaining probate, not least because that is what the legal profession would have us believe. It was not. There were hiccups, of course, but none of any great consequence. The process didn't take long, and it was not expensive. Anyone of reasonable intelligence, who can use a computer, write letters, keep accurate records, and understand official guidance should be perfectly capable of obtaining grant of probate and administering an estate.

This is a diary of what happened to me. It is not a typical 'How To' guide, but is a record of my personal experience. I hope it will encourage others to take the plunge.

www.ingramcontent.com/pod-product-compliance
Ingram Content Group UK Ltd.
Pitfield, Milton Keynes, MK11 3LW, UK
UKHW020231250726
13967UKWH00001B/310

9 780993 198724